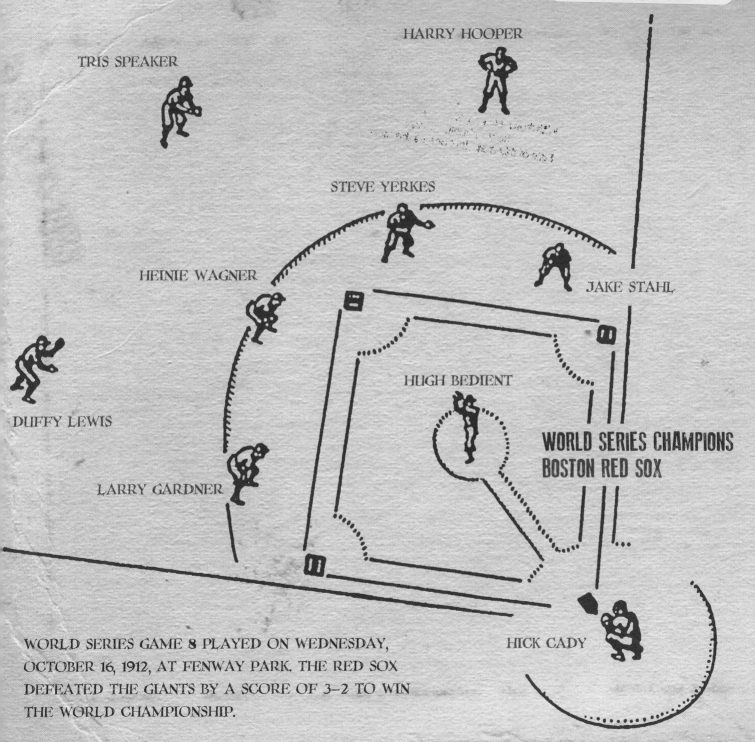

TRIS SPEAKER

HARRY HOOPER

STEVE YERKES

HEINIE WAGNER

JAKE STAHL

DUFFY LEWIS

HUGH BEDIENT

**WORLD SERIES CHAMPIONS
BOSTON RED SOX**

LARRY GARDNER

HICK CADY

WORLD SERIES GAME 8 PLAYED ON WEDNESDAY, OCTOBER 16, 1912, AT FENWAY PARK. THE RED SOX DEFEATED THE GIANTS BY A SCORE OF 3–2 TO WIN THE WORLD CHAMPIONSHIP.

WORLD SERIES CHAMPIONS

BOSTON RED SOX

SARA GILBERT

Published by Creative Paperbacks
P.O. Box 227, Mankato, Minnesota 56002
Creative Paperbacks is an imprint of The Creative Company
www.thecreativecompany.us

Design and production by Blue Design (www.bluedes.com)
Art direction by Rita Marshall
Printed in the United States of America

Photographs by Corbis (Bettmann), Getty Images (APA, Al Bello,
Bruce Bennett Studios, Diamond Images, Steve Dunwell, Elsa,
Focus on Sport, FPG, Jeff Gross, Otto Greule Jr./Allsport, Drew
Hallowell, Andy Hayt, Carl Iwasaki/Time & Life Pictures, G.
Newman Lowrance, Brad Mangin/MLB Photos, National Baseball
Hall of Fame Library/MLB Photos, Gary Newkirk, Rich Pilling/
MLB Photos, Photo File, Jim Rogash, Mark Rucker/Transcendental
Graphics, Joseph Scherschel/Time & Life Pictures, Ezra Shaw,
Brian Snyder-Pool, Rick Stewart, Ron Vesely/MLB Photos)

Library of Congress Cataloging-in-Publication Data
Gilbert, Sara.
Boston Red Sox / Sara Gilbert.
p. cm. — (World series champions)
Includes bibliographical references and index.
Summary: A simple introduction to the Boston Red Sox major
league baseball team, including its start in 1901, its World Series
triumphs, and its stars throughout the years.
ISBN 978-1-60818-260-2 (hardcover)
ISBN 978-0-89812-811-6 (pbk)
1. Boston Red Sox (Baseball team)—History—Juvenile literature. I.
Title.
GV875.B62G56 2013
796.357'640974461—dc23   2011051187

First edition
9 8 7 6 5 4 3 2 1

Cover: First baseman Adrian Gonzalez
Page 2: Left fielder Ted Williams
Page 3: Pitcher Jonathan Papelbon
Right: Catcher Carlton Fisk

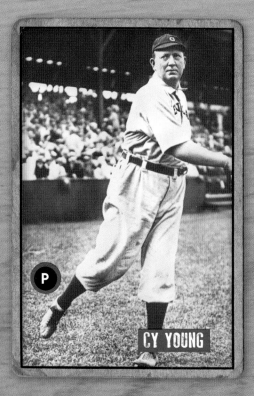

P

CY YOUNG

P

PEDRO MARTINEZ

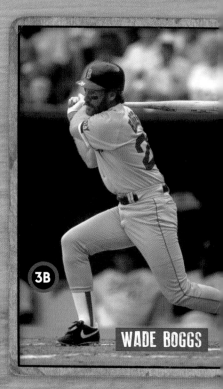

3B

WADE BOGGS

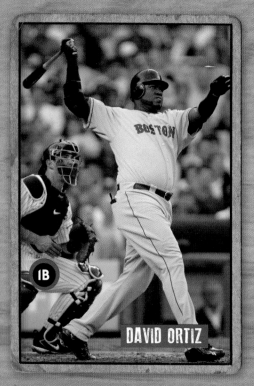

1B

DAVID ORTIZ

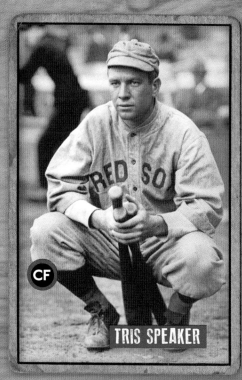

CF

TRIS SPEAKER

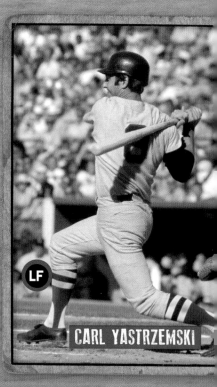

LF

CARL YASTRZEMSKI

TABLE OF CONTENTS

BOSTON AND FENWAY PARK

Boston is the **CAPITAL** of
Massachusetts. It is one of the
oldest cities in the United States.
Boston also has one of the oldest
ballparks. Since 1912, Fenway Park
has been the home of a baseball
team called the Red Sox.

AMERICAN LEAGUE											
P		1	2	3	4	5	6	7	8	9	H
25 PHILA.	2	0	0	1	0						7
33 BOSTON	2	0	0	1	2						6
26 WASH.	0	0	0	0	1						
21 NEW YORK	2	0	0	3	0						

FENWAY PA

BALL (H) STRII

OUT (E) AT B

AMERICAN LEAGUE
1 2 3 4 5 6 7 8 9 10

CHICAGO
ST.LOUIS
DETROIT
CLEVE.

NATIONAL LEAGUE
IN R   IN R
BOSTON 5 9   ST.LOUIS 1 0
PHILA. 1   CHICAGO 0
NEWYORK 1 0   CINN.
BROOK. 1   PITTS.

HERE TO-MORROW
WASH.

RIVALS AND COLORS

The Red Sox are 1 of 30 Major League Baseball teams. All the teams try to win the World Series to become world champions. Boston is a fierce **RIVAL** of the New York Yankees. The Red Sox wear red and white uniforms.

PITCHER JON LESTER

CATCHER JASON VARITEK

RIVALS AND COLORS

RED SOX HISTORY

The Red Sox played their first season in 1901. They were one of the best teams right away. The Red Sox won the very first World Series in 1903. Then they won 4 more in the next 15 years!

1903 WORLD SERIES

EMERSON SHOE

HUNTINGTON AVENUE BASE BALL GROUNDS

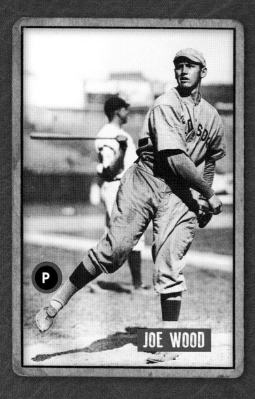

P

JOE WOOD

CF

DOM DiMAGGIO

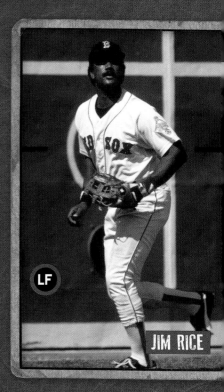

LF

JIM RICE

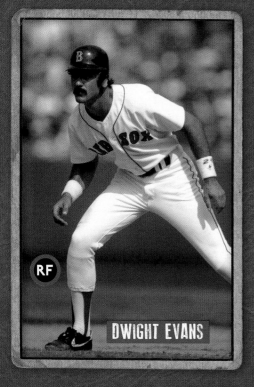

RF

DWIGHT EVANS

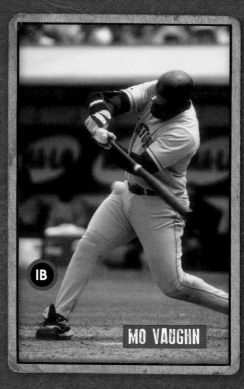

1B

MO VAUGHN

C

VICTOR MARTINEZ

BABE RUTH

In 1918, slugging outfielder Babe Ruth led Boston to its fifth championship. But then he was traded to the Yankees. After Ruth left, the Red Sox did not win the World Series for 86 years.

MANNY RAMIREZ

The Red Sox lost the World Series in 1946, 1967, and 1975. In 1986, they were one out away from winning. Then a ball slipped through the first baseman's legs. They lost again.

In 2004, powerful outfielder Manny Ramirez and big first baseman David Ortiz helped end Boston's DROUGHT. The Red Sox won the World Series in four straight games. They did that again in 2007, too!

DAVID ORTIZ

CY YOUNG

TED WILLIAMS

RED SOX STARS

Cy Young was an early Boston star. He pitched for the Red Sox
from 1901 to 1908 and won many games. An award for the
best pitcher in the league was named after him. Outfielder Ted
Williams played in the 1940s and '50s. Many people think he was
the greatest hitter ever.

Shortstop Nomar Garciaparra hit 30 home runs as a **ROOKIE** in 1997. He always **HUSTLED** on the field. Pitcher Pedro Martinez joined the Red Sox in 1998. He won two Cy Young Awards.

In 2007, second baseman Dustin Pedroia won the Rookie of the Year award. The next year, he won the Most Valuable Player award! The Red Sox hoped Pedroia would help them win more championships soon!

NOMAR GARCIAPARRA

DUSTIN PEDROIA

HOW THE RED SOX GOT THEIR NAME

The Red Sox were named for the socks they wore with their uniforms. Their socks were bright red. The team was called the Red Stockings at first. But then the owner shortened it to Red Sox. He liked the shorter name and thought it looked better in the newspaper.

CENTER FIELDER JACOBY ELLSBURY

ABOUT THE RED SOX

First season: 1901

League/division: American League, East Division

World Series championships:

1903	5 games to 3 versus Pittsburgh Pirates
1912	4 games to 3 versus New York Giants
1915	4 games to 1 versus Philadelphia Phillies
1916	4 games to 1 versus Brooklyn Robins
1918	4 games to 2 versus Chicago Cubs
2004	4 games to 0 versus St. Louis Cardinals
2007	4 games to 0 versus Colorado Rockies

Red Sox Web site for kids:

http://mlb.mlb.com/bos/fan_forum/kids_index.jsp

Club MLB:

http://web.clubmlb.com/index.html

GLOSSARY

CAPITAL — the city where a state's laws are made

DROUGHT — in baseball, a long time without winning

HUSTLED — moved fast or tried hard to get a job done

RIVAL — a team that plays extra hard against another certain team

ROOKIE — an athlete playing his or her first year

INDEX